COLLECTIVE THOUGHTS
OF A BLACK MAN

COLLECTIVE THOUGHTS OF A BLACK MAN

Hard Hitting Street Essays, Poems and Short Stories

SAEED MUHAMMED

Published by G Publishing, LLC

Cover Design: SOS Graphics and Designs

Editor: Francene Ambrose-Gunn

ISBN: 0-9788536-8-7

Library of Congress Control Number: 2006934951

Published and printed in the United States of America

www.gpublishingsuccess.com

DEDICATION

This book is dedicated to my family. Over the years, I have been blessed with strength, health and the gift of enlightenment, but the most precious gift I have received is my family. Thank you for your love, honesty, respect and spiritual power.

In Memory of:
   The Most Honorable Elijah Muhammed
   Frederick Douglass
   The Honorable Marcus M. Garvey
   Kwame Ture
   Minister Malcolm X
   Huey P. Newton (B.P.P.)
   Medgar Evers
   Fred Hampton (B.P.P.)
   Dr. Betty Shabazz
   Dr. Theda Bishop (Friend)

Your words of truth, your wisdom and your love for self and your people will never be forgotten.

May Peace be upon you,

BROTHER SAEED MUHAMMED

Holy Qur'an
Surah (15:26 through 29)

And surely we created man of sounding clay, of Black mud fashioned into shape And the jinn, we created before of Intensely hot fire.
And then thy Lord said unto the Angels, "I am going to create a mortal of sounding clay, of Black mud fashioned into shape.
So when I have made him of my spirit, fall down making obeisance to him."

Jinn: Any of a class of spirits, lower than the Angels, capable of appearing in human and animal forms, influencing humankind for good and evil.

Obeisance: A bow or curtsy, expressing deep respect or deferential courtesy — homage

ACKNOWLEDGMENTS

First, I must give praise to Allah (god). Without him giving me direction, wisdom and his love, I would have fallen prey to all the predators who seek to gain power any and every way they can.

Next, to my family, you mean more to me than I would ever express, especially my mother, The Queen Mother, who proved the so-called experts wrong when they said that a Black Woman could not raise, teach and guide a young black man by herself. I want them to know that even though I fly solo, the shadow above my head is not a black cloud. Instead, it is the ever present wing spread and power of your love that I fly beneath.

To my publisher and publicist, Sister J. Hunter, God led us to one another and I know that with each other, we will soar higher than we could ever imagine.

Last, but never least, to my Uncle Jimmy, your physical presence has ascended to a higher level, but your spirit, strength, and love still adds fuel to my fire, and I know that with your eyes looking down upon me, I hope I have made you proud.

Much love and respect to you all,

Brother Saeed Muhammed

PREFACE

First, I must state that I am not speaking for all black men. Next, throughout my life, I have experienced many harsh realities; some were by visual observations, while others have been physical and mental lessons. All in all, there is one lesson that has been superimposed on my mind. No matter how many of my brothers who speak of change, or say they support a particular movement that will push for the acknowledgement and respect for us as a strong black nation, many of them will simply fall by the curbside allowing others to continue to dictate to them the way that they should live, speak and think.

Therefore, I was forced to realize that in this war of injustice that has been thrust upon us, thousands of soldiers would die, while the remaining

millions of us will prevail. So, if at anytime during your reading of this book, you think or believe that this material is **raw, severe,** or **controversial**, I'm here to tell you that it is plain and simple. We can no longer afford to sit back and say in time things will get better, when we know just the opposite. We must stop sitting in our homes thinking quietly about the things that we desire most when it comes to change. We should speak, and speak loudly. As a people of great strength, we can no longer be afraid to speak because we are worried about what others will think or possibly take from us. Let's face it, you own nothing save your own soul. At this moment, our concerns should be that upon leaving this planet, we should depart with dignity, honor, and a sense of self. In conclusion, I would like to state that if this book brings about a change in your thoughts **(hopefully a positive change)** then I have done my job in spreading the truth, at least as I see it.

PEACE OUT

TABLE OF CONTENTS

AMERIKA

What is America? Land of the free? Home of the brave? Or is it mom's apple pie, baseball, hotdogs and a house with a white picket fence? My answer, **bullshit!**

First, let's take this land of the free jazz. You allowed your so-called forefathers to cross the ocean to take me from a home where I was being groomed to become a King, a Pharaoh or a great Warrior. Instead, I became a slave; someone who would pick your crops, raise your children, and even become your whipping toy when you wanted pleasure. Even today, when I'm suppose to be free, I must receive your approval to open my own business, to educate my children or to retire from a job where I gave you many years of service. So am I free? **Hell no!**

Next, what is this crap about mom's apple pie, baseball & hot dogs. First of all, my brother and I had to watch our mother work very hard to give us the things that we needed in order to survive, so if we needed apple pie, our best bet was to grab a frozen Sara Lee pie, bless it and be on our way.

Now about baseball. Hell, as far as I'm concerned, you could have kept this game seeing that you didn't want any of my brothers to be involved in it anyway. You even tried to deny our brothers who played in the Negro Leagues, by saying that our league was not a real league with real players, but that didn't stop us. Thanks to the efforts of Jackie Robinson, Satchell Paige, Hank Aaron and others; and today, the younger brothers are showing you up and collecting the big paychecks.

So why the barriers? Now, this hot dog thing! I don't even know where you got this from. You took that nasty **SWINE** and mixed it up with all types of other animals, then you gave us that filth to eat and when we survived eating it, you made it one of your favorite foods. Just like **CHITLINS** right?

Now, finally the almighty picket fence, white at that!!! Have you ever seen a picket fence in the ghetto? Hell no, and if you did, it's because one of my bewildered brothers or sisters watched too much of the Andy Griffith Show or Happy Days on television. How in the hell do you expect some of our brothers and sisters to have a fence when they can't even afford the house that stands behind it. Besides why be closed in, a fence is just another way of keeping me in prison, I'm suppose to be free, remember?

By now, I guess you are wondering why I spelled Amerika the way that I did. Well, as I see it, I helped build this country with my blood and strength, I'm told if need be, I must fight for it, and as far as leaving, I might as well stay here because you are trying to take control of my Mother-Land (Afrika) and make it just like this country. So the least you can do is allow me to spell Amerika the way that I would like to so that I can have something to remind me of home.

ONE MILLION PLUS ME

It was 5:05 a.m.; early morning. So early, the birds had not begun to sing. Yet, there was a noise. The sound, you ask? The sound was buses stopping, of men stretching and yawning, and cars coming to a halt. Where are all these men going, and where did they all come from? They came from all over; all fifty states, plus many other continents. They were headed to one destination, with one agenda, to prove one point.

I stood among them, marching like the street soldier I had always been. Only this time I was not just marching against injustice, for equal rights or unity; or for the atonement of others. No, this time I was marching for all those things, but most of all I was marching for me!

As the sun came up, I became amazed. I became awestruck at what was right there before my eyes. Right there in Washington D.C., the backyard and playground of Washington's so-called elite. I stood tall, proud and humble. I stood there with **One Million Black Men!** can you imagine that!!! One million men, all there for the same purpose--Unity, Atonement & Respect. I knew then that the rest of America had to wake up and realize that their worst nightmare had just come true. Here it was all these men standing at attention, standing strong, standing at peace with one another. As I stood there with these men, I felt, for once in my life, I didn't have to be aggressive or stand alert. I knew I was among my brothers and that I was my brother's keeper and he mine.

So, in conclusion, America, you better stand at attention and remain alert, because if you should ever feel as though you need to disrespect, mislead, or try to suppress my brothers and I again, we will once again come to attention, standing post, ready for the word. But next time the word may not be **PEACE.** So remember that dream, and remember that I am, in fact, my brother's keeper, and he is most surely mine!

"THANK YOU"

A TRIBUTE TO MOMMA

T hank you for bringing me into this world. Thank you for raising me, loving me teaching me, and even whipping me when I needed it. Thank you for clothing and feeding me. But most importantly, thank you for grooming me to become a strong and powerful Black man. It is because of you that I became the man I am today.

Through your eyes and heart, I was taught that a man should always respect his woman, children and most of all **HIMSELF.** Thank you for allowing me to face the world and bump my head, when I really knew all along that you were standing in the shadows ready to protect me at any cost.

Momma, Clair Huxtable (The Cosby Show) has nothing on you, and I would not have asked or

wished for any other mother. Momma, if I could I would give you the world, but knowing you, just settling for the best that I could give would be fine with you. So momma, I give you all of my love and respect, but most of all I give you my everlasting and most gracious
THANK YOU.

LOOKING INWARD

When searching for our destiny
we must possess Morals, Values and Positive Beliefs.
But first, we must create a thought process
that will enable us to project respect
for one another and for self.
We must come together as a Strong,
Self-Sufficient,
Self-Sustaining
Black Nation.

PEACE BE UPON YOU...

S. K. W.

A DEDICATION of LOVE

When I close my eyes, I can see your bright smile.
When I open my heart, I can feel your warm touch.
When I look out onto this troubled world and I become sad,
I think of you and my world is at peace.
You make my days bright,
My cold mornings warm,
But most of all you put my heart & soul at peace.

Love Always,
ME....

I'LL RISE

Today's ignorance and racially illicit verbal and physical maltreatment of my people cannot be justified by the fact that you did not grow-up with or around black people. Or by the fact that it is your fore fathers, along with those other **SHEET-HEADS** (The Klan) of America, who continue to try to keep my people and their accomplishments out of the History Books. But that's all right. **I'LL RISE.**

It is also time for you to stop using that tired excuse that everything that you have learned, seen or heard about black people has come from reading a book (that was written by liars), watching TV, the movies, or the News Media. Hell, if they did not receive their information from the black community it was wrong anyway. If you are that curious, why don't you come and talk to me. But if you choose not to, it's no great lost to me. Believe me, **I'LL RISE.**

But there are a few things I would like you to understand. I'll Rise over any and all adversity. I'll Rise above every conflict that you could present. I'll rise above any negative convictions that you may have towards me, I'll even rise up in death. It's plain and simple, **I'LL RISE, I'LL RISE, I HAVE I CAN AND I WILL CONTINUE TO RISE.**

A TRIBUTE TO BLACK HEROES

You gave your life so that many of us would receive Equality, Respect and a better chance at living in peace. Within the time of your life, you took on all of the harsh verbal and physical mistreatment directed at us simply because of our skin color. With your death, you left behind a great legacy, abundance of knowledge, philosophies and teachings to be passed on. What would this world and some of our people be like had you not lived? What would I have become without having your great influence in my life?

Thank you Dr. King for your dreams. Thank you Marcus Garvey for your philosophies of life. Thank you Minister Malcolm X. for your perseverance and self-knowledge, and I thank you Most Honorable Elijah Muhammed, for all of your teachings on man, the World and all that revolves around almighty, Allah.

Thank you to all of my brothers who have died, so that all of us could live! All that you have left behind can be obtained with greatest of ease and applied so that this history of ours will not cease to exist. I just hope that all of my brothers today will wake-up and put these legacies to use.

THE ANSWER IS

I was asked the question
What is life?
My answer was
Life is a child daydreaming, visualizing a destiny that
will surely come.
Life is setting a goal to claim the universe, only to
fall short upon the stars,
  but still realizing that your achievements are still
great and high.
Life is the sun, when it's shining down on a playful
child.
Happiness.

FOR A BRIEF MOMENT

A man is just a man,
But without woman,
A man is like the sun when it's going down
There is only darkness.
Man has prevailed over other men,
Standing tall while receiving showers of awards and
being labeled great.
But when it comes to woman,
A man must be humble,
Realizing that it is her strength and beliefs in her
man
That truly makes him a King.
As a man I can stand on a Mountain Top
With my head held high towards the sky,
But without my woman by my side
For me to acknowledge her part in helping me
achieve my goals,
I would only be great
FOR A BRIEF MOMENT

TWO HOMES, BUT ONE HEART

East is where home was. West is where home is now! East was where the first man and woman were created, lived and shared a life in the Garden of Eden. West is where man has tried to create his own Eden.

East is where the warm sun's rays beam down on the children, and where they can run and play **FREELY** in paradise. West is where the concrete jungle is; where the children run, but not playing freely or the warm sunrays. They run because the only things that are beaming down on them are the sights at the end of a **gun** as they receive showers of bullets.

East was the beginning, could west be the end? West is where America is, and the place where I was born; a place that offers me freedom in a physical form (but we know that has not always been true. But America, I want inner peace. Peace in my mind where I can be and perform as a whole man and not be restricted or castigated for my beliefs, values and or wants.

Africa is east, where a child is born and prepared for his *Rights of Passage* into manhood. A place where inner and outer peace reflects one. **MAN AND ALLAH (GOD) ARE UNIFIED.** Africa you are my roots of origin. I've never met you, but I plan to. Though your children were taken from you so long ago, and even though many of us, your children, know nothing about you, our Motherland can never be taken from our **SOULS.**

So I will end by saying," *The child has left home, but the home has never left the child."*

WAKE-UP, RE-GROUP & STAND STRONG

Blackman
You must not allow others to inflict you
With false hope and pride.
My brothers,
The belly of the beast is a bottomless pit.
Blackman,
You must wake-up
From this self-induced sleep,
You must stand at attention,
Protecting your family, home, and self.
There is a required need for the black man.
So as brothers
Let us re-group and re-claim
Our respected place in History.
Brothers
If we don't stay on our path to glory
We will surely head down the path toward
DESTRUCTION!!!
But most of all

We will also take our beloved brothers and sisters down
That deadly path that will lead to
GENOCIDE...

PROMISE

MY DEDICATION TO S.K.W.

My promise to you is my love,
To listen when you speak,
To feel when you touch.
My promise to you is the warmth of my heart,
And the strength of my soul.
My promise to you is
To take all of your tears and
Turn them into showers of joy,
To take your fears and replace them with hope,
Assurance and the belief in me.
My promise to you is that I take your Heart & Soul
And protect them with that of mine,
To let you know that if any danger were to arise
I would protect your life
Even if this means I would lose **mine.**

Collective Thoughts of a Black Man

FORGOTTEN LEGACY

If the father does not teach the son about his **HISTORY** or **HERITAGE,** all is lost. When it's time for the son of the father to teach the grandson about his **HISTORY & HERITAGE,** all is long gone, because both have ceased to exist. Man is gone because he has forgotten where he came from. His history is gone because he did not take the time to pass on the rich and fulfilling legacy. Now, the son must struggle to create a false history, which leaves the grandson in a state of disillusionment, unable to focus in on the true meaning of **Family, Fatherhood,** and just being that proud and powerful Black man that his people and culture once produced and groomed.

MEASURELESS

Stop Trying To Measure Me Up

A man cannot be measured by his woman, his people, or solely upon the impact of his accomplishments alone. For man, his personal best is a great accomplishment.

It's not the number of things he has done that counts, but the intensity of each of his endeavors. What man becomes while roaming on earth will evolve from his friends & foes. Those he loved and those who loved him. Those he reached out and touched and those who reached back to touch him. Those he gave to and those he took from.

But it is by the grace of **ALLAH** (who is the source greater than man himself), not his woman or his people, that man does exist.

BLACK QUEEN

Black Queen, your hair shines as bright as a moonlit night.

Your skin is as soft as the finest silks that were presented to the pharaohs as gifts.

Black Queen, you are as pure to me as the great river Euphrates is to the Egyptians.

Black Queen, your eyes show love, trust, hope and our destiny.

Your soul has strength, confidence and support for family and yourself.

You are truly one of God's most precious gifts to this world, and in my opinion,

of the *Seven Wonders of the World*, you are the second,

Only because Almighty Allah is first in my life.

All praises be to Allah, for giving me such a rare jewel as the **BLACK QUEEN.**

NEVER

As a **Black man**
I'm suppose to be chained and shackled
by things such as poverty and the lack of
opportunities that may come my way,
or just by the fact that I am black.

As a **Black man**
I've been confused.
Over the years I have been called
Darkie, Nigger, Negro, Colored, Black Afro-American, African-American
then **Black** again.
Now do you see my point?!!!
Why can't I just be addressed as
Sir, Mister, or better yet, just as a **Man.**

As a **Black man**
I'm suppose to look-up to and respect
those who try to **Enslave** me with the power
that they only think or imagine they have.
I want to leave them with this thought;

their **Chains** I have broken,
the **Shackles** that remain on my wrists
are not there to remind me of where I've been,
but to remind me of where
I refuse to **Return.**

Collective Thoughts of a Black Man

OLD GLORY

Many times I would sit and stare out of my office window thinking about my plight in life, and the dilemma of my people. Then the wind would shift. I could tell even with the windows closed because far away on top of a building, flapped what some would call **OLD GLORY**. A piece of cloth sewn together with stars and stripes by an old woman sitting on her porch (or so we were told).

For many years, I listened to certain people say that this flag represents the people and it's country. But how could this be? This flag castigated my people, then and now. Every twenty-five years someone has to sign for the approval of our civil rights. We must stand and pay tribute to it even though we are treated as second-class citizens under this same flag. Hell, even the N.B.A. **(National Basketball Association)** line their pockets with a brother's hard-earned cash by giving out fines just because one of their players would not stand and acknowledge the real purpose of this flag. It's **"Liberty for some, justice for a few, but not a damn thing for you and me."** If my brother's did not show-up to entertain the people, there would be no basketball anyway. Now somebody run and tell that to Commissioner David Stern. The way I see it, there should be a new flag; one that represents us all. **Native-American/Black/Asian/Chinese/ Japanese/Arab/Latino,** oh, and of course, let's not forget about **White America.**

WORDS MEAN EVERYTHING

GONE -- Is all of the dreams that you once dreamed.

TRAPPED -- In a Community that is influenced by hopelessness and negativity. **OPPRESSED -- By** a society that does not give a damn if I live or die.

SUPPRESSED -- By the feelings that every time I make a positive move towards advancing in life, I maybe watched or put in check.

SET-UP -- By the so-called **Master Race** or by the **Hidden Government**, to fail at whatever I may try to achieve in life.

GENOCIDE -- Can't allow it, won't allow it. My people mean much too much to me.

FIGHT BACK -- We have too much to lose. Lives, History, but most of all a Generation that follows.

FREEDOM -- NEED I SAY MORE!!!!!!!!!!!!!!!!!!!!!!!!!!

JUSTICE

What is Justice?

Does this word have any meaning to it anymore, or is it a luxury for a choice few.

Is justice a plaything for the rich, a wish-filled want for the poor?

Will the majority of cases continue to be lopped sided, meaning that when a white man walks out of court he will say, **"Justice was served for me?"**

While a black man walks out of court saying, **"Just Prison awaits me."**

So does this mean that the Rich will continue to receive justice?

The Middle Class (or the well off) will continue to be justified by justice,

While the poor continue to say, **"It's just us waiting for our turn at Justice…"**

MOVING FORWARD

One must take the proper steps in life to prepare for his or her destiny.

In doing so, the mind must be as strong, or stronger than the body.

The more that you are motivated to give 100% in every endeavor,

The more likely you are to create the kind of intensity it takes to build

A Great Mind & Soul.

RELATIONSHIP

We give and we take
We ask and we receive
We like, but yet we don't love
Is this a relationship?
We seek, but what is it that we are looking for?
We ask and we say that we know,
But we have yet to learn.
We say to each other that we love one another,
But still we have doubts
In the end we move on,
But still we say I'll always be here.

IS THIS A RELATIONSHIP?

F. E. A. R.
(False Evidence Appearing Real)

White man, why is it that you fear me? Why do you try to separate me from my family, friends and brothers? But most of all, why do you try to get me to fight against myself with the drugs that you brought into this country?

You have attacked me from every angle that you could think of and still I remain right here in front of you.

White man, you've tried to erase my History. You even tried to brainwash me by teaching your fake history. But instead, you have shown and proven to me just how dirty you are, and you gave me more power to use against you -- **Knowledge.**

If I am dangerous, it is not because of the reasons that you give,

"Not Educated, Criminal Minded, and cannot be trusted."

By all means, it's just the opposite. I'm far more capable of retaining more in my mind than you'll ever be aware of, and as far as **history** is concerned, the majority of history is linked to my Mother Land and our people.

So if there is anything that makes me dangerous, it is the positive things about being black that strikes fear inside of you.

Pride/Strength/History/Respect for ones self and others. And last, to be able to endure all of the **Bull Shit** that you have put on my people and me for over 440 years.

So if you are afraid of me, and you should be, I am the force that will not be **destroyed.**

TO LOVE A BLACK WOMAN

To love a Black Woman, means that I must drink from the very essence that made her a Black Queen, so that I could love, support and understand her in every way that a black woman should be cared for.

To love a Black Woman, means that I should taste the tears that she cries when she shows signs of fear, to reassure her that I would cross the deepest river and hottest desert to prove my love and to acknowledge to the world that she is mine.

To love a Black Woman, means that I can give her possession of my soul and still represent myself as a strong Black Man to those who dare challenge me.

To love a Black Woman, means that our foreplay would consist of me caressing her heart, making love to her mind, and finally, to bring her soul to an earth shaking climax,

To love a Black Woman means that I should quote
Barry White by saying,
"My, My, My".

AS THE WORLD TURNS

My eyes are open, but my world is closed.
The nature of my being is man, but I feel like a child,
Lost.
The world and its people are changing,
People are growing older and the world is in a mode of **DESTRUCTION,**
 But the game remains the same
VIOLENCE-DEATH-POVERTY and
   the **STRUGGLE TO BE FREE...**

Collective Thoughts of a Black Man

I COULD HAVE BEEN, BUT I WOULD RATHER BE

I could have been like Dr. King, preaching that "I Have A Dream" and fighting for **CIVIL RIGHTS**, but I would rather be like Malcolm X teaching his brothers and sisters about perseverance and fighting for **HUMAN RIGHTS.**

I could have been one of those many Candidates who seek a powerful political office and make promises that I would break or lie about in front of Millions of people.

But I would rather be a strong, intelligent, powerful Blackman that would stand before more than a Million of his brothers to deliver a message of *love, gratification, hope* and make a sincere promise to continue to up lift his people as Minister Louis Farrakhan did before a stunned, open mouthed, non-believing American Society.

I could have been one of those scared, cowardly house Negroes who told Mister Charlie everything just to keep shoes on his feet and eat warm leftover cornbread

(I really doubt it). But more realistically, I would have been one of those brothers who would have escaped every chance I got. Or better yet, I would have led the revolt against the so-called Master Race.

I could have been like Michael Jordan or Deon Sanders with the big money salaries and cool T.V. commercials, but I would rather be a Teacher, to educate our children, and to know that I've done my very best when I see one of my students become a success.

I could have been one of those brothers who hung out and played the field with many different women and no children. Instead, I'm happy to know that I have a beautiful wife and daughter to come home to, and believe me it's a wonderful joy.

I could have been many things, but at last, I would rather be all the things that I've become, but more importantly,

I'm proud just to be **ME!**

JEALOUSY

What is it that makes other races afraid of mine? What is it that makes another man hate me because of my skin color? What makes you think that when you put down my Black Queen or try to take her from me, that I will not fight or be willing to die for her, so that she will continue to be respected.

What makes you think that I cannot be a good father to my children in the same context that you only pretend to be with yours?

Answers! For one, your weak souls can no longer handle the fact that what you did to my ancestors, and what you try to continue to use against me today, will no longer be allowed. Second, I can only imagine that when you look at the beauty of my black skin, you see eternal youthfulness. You wish and dream that your skin would glisten in the sun the way that mine does.

Next, is this situation with my Queen. I've figured out your plot. When you put her down, it's because you are hurt or because you really want her by your side. Now you should know by now that a Queen will never leave her King, especially not for the likes of you. But you still try to anger me and establish some kind of war.

Last, my children. Now, this is an area only a fool would explore, **(but look at who I'm talking to anyway)**. I will do what ever is necessary and in my power to provide for them, and see they are treated with respect and equality. Besides, it is my duty and a honor to pave the pathway for the next rulers of my kingdom.

So as I see it, you hate disrespect, and fear, for one simple reason, my blackness represents **UNITY, POWER & DIGNITY,** but most of all, the **Uniqueness** that no other race can make a claim to, **GENESIS,** the beginning.

WHEN YOU HAVE LOST HER

A Relationship that's Gone

I said things that should not have been said.
I said things that could have been worded another way.
I've accused when there was nothing to be accused of.
I had taken a soft and gentle loving person and made her cold, just as I am.
But now I've disassembled myself spiritually, mentally, physically and soulfully, to rebuild.
To show myself that I am and can be that person she once loved.
I'm just about complete.
I've put myself back together with only a few insecurities.
For a man, just as all other men, it's natural to have some fears.
It is that fear that keeps me alive in tough situations.

But I have learned that I can leave that behind when I'm with the person that I love.

So, when the program's completed, I will be that person she once loved, respected and felt confident in, and maybe our love can again fly past all of the boundaries that they once soared over.

But if it's too late, then hopefully, love will find it's way back to me, and

I will be sure not to make the same mistakes.

PAY ATTENTION

The Black man is not a **Criminal-Minded, Lack-Luster, Child Abandoning, Non-Educated** male, who's only purpose in life is to self-destruct and destroy his race. That is just the picture that some of White America has painted for those people who do not know any better.

Instead, the Black man is the main focal point of his people. One who, when chosen, will rise to the occasion to lead his race from the depths of a man-made hell, to the promised land of **Equality, Honor and Greatness.**

This same Black man has died, and will die again; not to show that he was some kind of hero. He died to prove to many that his death would be more meaningful if his people continued to strive for what he stood for in life. He chose to die rather than to live and watch his people take all of his teachings and wash them down the drain.

And because of this, when a people stand as one, unify, and continue to pass down the positive teachings that they have learned early in life, one question should be asked?

Now that you've killed the lion, what do you do with his cubs?

COME FORTH

Will the Real Black man Step Forth

Black man, now that the truth has been exposed, will you please step-up.

Black man, the truth was told to us by Brother Malcolm X.

"We've been took, we've been had, bamboozled and hoodwinked," and still we continue to settle for what America has given us-**NOTHING.**

Black man, knowing that all of these things have happened to us, how can we sit back any longer.

It's time! **Please come forth!**

Black man, within our strengths, pride, history & heritage is a unique force

That is waiting for us to bring it to light. That force is **UNITY.**

Within our unity, the picture may reflect thousands, but the reality reflects **ONE!**

Black man, please stand-up and stand proud.

Please speak-up and speak loud, but most of all realize that the time has come for us, **the Black men to come forth...**

KING DIONTE AND PRINCE RESHAWN

My Promise to You

Born into a world of violence and beasts of burden were the two new rays of hope. Two beautiful black children who will become the next rulers of our kingdom. They will spend many years of their lives being taught the true **HISTORY** of their people. They will spend many hours in training, preparing to become warriors. Both will be groomed in matters of respect for self and others, especially their elders, who took the time to lay this pathway for them.

How do I know the things I know? Because I am their watcher, protector and mentor. I am Pharaoh, and as Pharaoh, it is my job to prepare these young black children; to allow them to have fun, as all children should, and to teach them when a lesson needs to be taught. But most of all to lead them by a positive demonstration of walking with my head held high, my chest built up with power and pride, and my mind filled with a legacy that no man can take from me.

Last, King Dionte and Prince Reshawn, my personal promise to you is to love and protect you both until I take my very last breath. And even in death, the strength of my soul shall continue to guide you down the right paths. So until then, I will sit proudly upon the highest rock like the mighty lion watching over his cubs, waiting for the time to come when you will take your rightful places upon your *thrones*.

UNCLE JIMMY

A Tribute to Walter N. Hatcher

You taught me about the streets and how not to become a victim of its predatory ways. You introduced me to the **HUSTLER'S MANUAL,** the ways and life styles of a Pimp, Dealer and dog in the streets. Of course this was the book that you wrote, voted number one by all of the students that you once tutored.

I thought I had completed your course and was on my way to becoming a Player, but you stood me up only to knock me back down, not physically, but verbally. You then told me to get an education and become somebody. When I asked why? You told me that a life in the streets is a short life, one day you are on top and the next day someone could be mowing the grass on your grave. You also said that you were fortunate to have been able to teach me these things. But your main reason for all of the lessons was, (and I quote you,) "that a man needs balance in his life. If he only has book knowledge, then the dogs in the streets will have a feast, and if a man only has street knowledge without having book sense, then he will be totally lost and will lose out on all of the benefits that a good life could offer him".

You also said something that I will never forget. You said that you wanted me to become better than you were in life. I say to you, thanks for all of the lessons about the streets. Thanks for guiding me towards the pathway of education. Thanks for teaching me about men like Martin, Malcolm, Marcus and Elijah.

I never got the chance to say, no matter what others may have thought of you, or what kind of person they said you were, I want you to know that I could never be better than you were in life. That's because you were then, and still now a friend, mentor, teacher and a hero. But most of all you will always be my **"UNCLE JIMMY"**

MAY YOUR SOUL REST IN PEACE…

MY SPECIAL PLACE

My mind wonders at times, and in this state of solitude I discover that I am traveling within myself. During these travels, I find peace, peace that takes me from all of the dangers of the streets and the sadness of the world.

A place where no one speaks harsh or threatening words, where I'm accepted as a man for all of my good qualities and not because I have bought my own space. A place where my skin color means nothing, but my heart and soul mean everything.
I am so grateful that I have this place, a spot that cannot be entered by others unless I allow them to come in. And when I decide to emerge and you notice that there is a brightness in my eyes, and a positive tone in my voice, I ask you to please do not bother me with your misery, gossip or any other

annoying things of life, but just for that brief moment please leave me alone, or better yet, leave me at peace.

Oh! That place that I've been talking about is my mind. Try traveling inside of yours.

I WONDER

Today I saw another one of my brothers shot and killed. No, I was not there on the spot, but that's the image I received after closing my eyes and listening to the news report of an unknown black man being killed. And the two men who shot this brother thought they were getting pleasure from firing a weapon. But when caught by the police, the only thing that they could say was, it was a bad mistake. So I wondered what were they thinking about and what would make them go out and shoot at someone.

Yesterday I heard one of my sisters agree to being called a **BITCH** and then she said, "Yes, I'm that bitch, the worst bitch that you'll ever meet!" So I wondered, what would happen if someone or some music video made the word whore (or street name **HOE**) glamorous, would she then say that she's sold her body more times than a quarter has been re-circulated. (Better check the year of that coin before answering)

Tomorrow I will probably see one of my younger brothers walking down the street with his pants hanging down to his knees, showing off his underwear. And again I will wonder if this brother were allowed to walk down the streets with just his Joe Boxers on, what would he do then?

The Sprite commercial says image means nothing, but taste means everything. I say your image is a part of you, and you are what you represent. But alas, I'm only one voice, so I guess I'll just continue to wonder.

28 Days

I was staring out of a window, deep in concentration, putting all of my thoughts in order for a lecture that I was about to deliver. Then, suddenly, there was a question that I had to ask myself. How can I give a complete picture of Black History in forty-five minutes? Then the answer came. The same way our people are to learn about their **greatness** in **28 days.**

Twenty-eight days taken from hundreds perhaps thousands of years. Twenty-Eight days to give honor to those who gave their lives and sacrificed their families. Twenty-eight days to learn about Black people that some are only hearing about today. We, as a nation of strong Black Kings and Queens, will no longer allow those who thought they were in control to continue to ration out information on our history and culture. It's time that we realize that we deserve more than **28 Days.**

I want you to remember this, we receive a recognized **28 Days** to come together as a nation, trying to solve our cultural and community problems, and to fight against the injustice that has been thrust upon us. And for **28 Days,** we as a people have to figure out how to undo the remaining **337 Days** of social, political and economical **BULLSHIT** that we will once again face. But of all things to remember while celebrating our History, try to add *to* history by becoming a Great Leader or Achiever, and believe me, it will take far more than **28 Days** to accomplish this.

SHATTERED IMAGES

I've seen his face before. His eyes are the same color as mine. His skin is the same as mine, and his total essence, is like mine. Strong, and intelligent, an offspring of Royalty, his Blackness can never be tested; his family unity can never be denied. He would rather die with honor, than live with dishonor.

Suddenly, his image starts to fade and tears run down my face like a waterfall flowing towards a deep river. The image that I once admired and respected, is now gone.

I never knew his name, or where he came from, but I do know that he was my brother, not by blood, but still my brother.

So where did he go? The truth might scare you. This brother fell into a **Self-Exile**. He committed the ultimate sin, **"SELF-DESTRUCTION."** He gave into all the pressures that life would provide, by running towards and eventually becoming a slave to **Poverty** and **Drugs.** His will was broken, his soul destroyed, his family is gone, and his Blackness means nothing, because he will sell his very essence to **Cop A Blow!!!!**

Black man what happened? You were never alone. I was there, and I am still here fighting the same wars that you once fought. Do not give in now. Do not leave your family, your History and Future. Most of all do not leave me. We can win this war of injustice and insanity, but I need your help. I need my strong Black brother. Come back. It's not too late, because this ultimate prize of **Freedom** will once again make the Black man **GREAT...**

BOBBY G.

A Father's Lesson to His Son

As a child, I was a very angry young man. Many times I presented an attitude that was dangerous, not only to me, but also to others who were around me at that moment. I thought this was associated with that fact that I did not have a father in my household. Most of my friends had fathers who lived at home. They would take their sons to sporting events and teach them about things that they would experience later in life. But I discovered later during my teen-aged years that the positive things I observed in some of my friends homes at certain moments were nothing more than simple *illusions*; a cover-up to hide the real internal problems of their families and households.

It was at this time that I decided to look at my father, but it was not until I decided to sit and talk to him as a man, **Face to Face,** that I learned the difference between *father* and *daddy*. My father told me that any man can meet a woman and help produce a child, but it takes a real man to be able to stand-up and face his responsibilities, which are taking care of his woman and child by providing for their physical and mental welfare. By being a role model and powerful influence, not only to his family, but also to those he will meet over his life. By being the best man he could possibly be, and some of the time, that would be my father.

My father was seldom there in a physical presence, but by occurrence he could be there mentally. My father never came to see me participate in any athletic events, but he did show up one time when I caused chaos in the classroom. When I wanted expensive gym shoes, he would not give me the time of day, but when my mother called to say that I needed dress shoes on my feet, then for that moment he came through like a champ.

My father did not teach me the little things, like how to shave, but he did give me a few pointers on how not to get your throat cut while hanging in the streets. I've learned from him survival, respect, some love, and a lot of self-determination. But most of all,

I learned the lesson he tried his best to teach, and that there are many reasons why a man is not to be able to live under the same roof with his family, but there are no reasons for him not to take care of them.

So what's my point? Well, just because a man has the title of **Daddy,** should he really deserve the role of **Father**, especially if he's not doing what he is empowered to do? **Think about it.**

Collective Thoughts of a Black Man

THE DARKSIDE

There was a time that, even with my eyes closed, I could see all my dreams forming into reality. My eyes are open now, but all I see is darkness.

My mind is blank and empty. I know that the dreams are still there, but somehow they have fallen into a black hole, hopefully to be released by a strong jolt of realness. I feel as though everything and everyone around me has changed, or that I have possibly changed.

What can I do, no what *must* I do to change it all back? All that I've known, cared about, and loved has disappeared. My personality and feelings have gone back to the way they use to be, stone cold, hard and now very dangerous. I must regain that feeling of hope. I have to pull all my dreams out of that black hole, somehow, to make them a reality again. Because if I don't, there will be a fight. **HOPE v. DESPAIR. DREAMS v. POSSIBLE FAILURE. THE GOOD IN ME v. THE POWER OF MY DARKSIDE.** It has to change. I was a gladiator fighting for the weak against all the injustices that has been thrown at those I love & care about. Now I'm a gladiator **battling myself.**

LONELY OR ALONE

When you don't have anyone to dream, laugh and cry with, then you are lonely. When you don't have anyone to talk about your problems with, or no one wants to express their problems to you, then you are real lonely. When you don't have someone there with you to remember those special times that you both shared together, then you are very lonely.

Face the realization that sometimes you must dream, cry and laugh by yourself, and that you are the only one who is best qualified to listen and solve your own problems. If you realize that all of those special times can become more meaningful just because you are sharing them with yourself, then you are not lonely. You are **ALONE**. And believe me, there is a difference.

Collective Thoughts of a Black Man 85

Collective Thoughts of a Black Man

US AND THEM

A Black and White Thing

We brought forth Philosophy, Religion and all true knowledge of History.
They brought forth the Ships, the Money and the Chains.

We brought forth Spirituality, Unity, Love for self and family.
They brought forth the Whips, the Trees, the Cotton and hatred for us and even themselves.

We brought forth Rhythm, Dance and Celebration.
They brought forth Thievery, Jealousy and Deception.

We brought forth Herbs and Roots to heal; what man know today as medicine.
They brought forth Man-Made drugs to cause pain Disillusionment and Mass Destruction.

Yesterday and today, we bring forth the will to survive.

Yesterday and tomorrow, they will continue to bring forth more Lies, Corruption and Death.

TO SAVE OUR FUTURE

We must continue to cultivate the minds of our younger brothers and sisters. In doing so, we must nourish their souls with food for their spiritual growth. We must have a strong and powerful love for their desiring hearts, and respect for their beliefs, values and moral choices in life.

In order to do this, we must first change and re-evaluate our own thinking from negative to positive. We should also re-claim what is rightfully ours, **History.**

Our next goal should be the re-construction of our communities, starting with the family, and then the neighborhoods, until we, as strong Black people, can function as one complete solid race, with **Unity.**

This is a definite requirement in order to prevent any further destruction of our culture.

After the re-building process is completed, our final goal should be to stop those who insist on stealing our **Legacy**. We must bring to an end to the trickery by those who constantly prey upon others who are weak and lack the understanding and concept of pride within one's self. Then, finally, we will be able to lift our Mighty Nation of Black Kings and Queens and place them back upon the thrones, where they truly belong....

PRECIOUS

She is more rare than the finest Gem and more valuable than the most expensive diamond in the world. She is strong and independent. She has raised our children and made our houses into homes. She continues to give love even if she does not receive love. She is the Black woman.

She believes in her Black Man, even though he has sometimes abandoned her for a false sense of pride, or for a **Fake Beauty** who has been cast out by her own race. The Black woman has been put down, beat down, and kicked around, yet she remains strong and untainted. The Black woman is a leader and a role model, a teacher, mother, sister, friend and queen.

The Black woman is a nourishing strength of life. Last, but never least, the Black woman is a

TREASURE, our treasure; someone who has brought a smile to my face when I was angry. Someone who has understood my plight in life when I did not understand it myself. The Black woman brings life. So to all my brothers, please let's not lose or let someone else take our Queens from us. We must do whatever is necessary and in our power to give her all the love and respect that is needed to make her happy because she is truly a treasure and truly **PRECIOUS...**

LEADERSHIP

What is leadership? Leadership is defined by Webster's dictionary as: (1) the position or function of a leader, (2) having the ability to lead, (3) an act or instance to lead. But is this the true definition for leadership? I say no!

There are so many other important components to add such as Values, Morals, Influence, Vision and Charisma. A leader must also have the ability to listen and feel for the needs of the people they are leading. One who leads should be able to empower his people to realize that a change is needed and that they (the people) have the power to make those changes.

When I think of vision as a quality for a leader, I must add that this leader should be able to see the future of his people, then be able to relate that future back to those he is leading, and have his people focus in on that future, right there in the present. Malcolm X once said, "Those that are best prepared for the future, prepare for it today." One of the most important qualities that a leader should have is Inner Strength to be able to stand with his people to the very end, regardless of the outcome.

When I put all of those qualities together I can give you a list of outstanding people, but instead I will give you three very strong leaders. Dr. Betty Shabazz, who kept her husband's (Malcolm X) dream of self-perseverance and Human Rights alive. I think of Corretta Scott King. As a leader, she keeps her husband's (Dr. Martin L. King, Jr.) dream of Civil Rights and Peace between all races alive. I think of Merlie Evers, who placed herself on the front line with those other two great women to battle all the injustice we face everyday. I'm very sure that her husband, Civil Rights legend, Medgar Evers, would be proud.

But most of all, we should think and consider ourselves leaders. To quote the words of The Honorable Louis Farrakhan, "If we look within ourselves, we will find our leaders."

So in conclusion, the next time that we come together to decide on who should be our leader(s), let's focus in on the things that are not in the dictionary that define a leader which are Values, Morals, Vision, Influence and Charisma before we give that person the powerful title, **LEADER.**

Collective Thoughts of a Black Man

A COMPLETED JOURNEY

Gifted are the children who can foresee their destiny.

Blessed are the children who will work hard and not allow anything to get in their way.

Rewarded are the children who can look back and realize that they may not have been born with silver spoons in their hands,

But when all is done their clouds will have silver linings and their pathways will be paved with gold.

In the end the hardships will turn to glory,

The sacrifices made will be rewarded with love, respect and honor.

The Journey is now complete…

UNDERCOVER BROTHER

THE STORY of YOUNG BLOOD

Check him out, standing there in his Brooks Brothers shoes, and his Hickey Freeman suit, checking the minutes on his Timex watch while clutching his dear, precious, briefcase for life. Young brothers walk by, not even noticing that he is alive, but you can bet your last dollar that he's watching them. Now he's on the move, trying to get out of his old neighborhood. The same hood that he played in as a young child, the hood that he made his reputation in as a ball player shooting hoops with the fellas from sun up till sun down, but most of all, it was that same hood that loved protected and supported him through his young life. And now that he's all grown up and has become successful, he wants to forget it all.

His friends who still live on that same old street didn't go to college, but they all have good jobs and they take good care of their families. Yet still they are not good enough for **Young Blood.**

Young Blood also wants to forget about his family. He says they embarrass him. But how soon did he forget it was his mom who worked up to sixty hours a week to put an extra twenty dollars in her bank account to cover his college tuition. It was also **Young Blood's** older brother and sister who gave up their chances of going to college to work in the factories, so that they could help put **Young Blood** through school. Still he says they embarrass him.

Young Blood has told people that his family is uneducated, loud and crude, that they lack the so-called "social refinement" that he is supposed to have. **Young Blood's** problem is that the only thing of importance to him is the approval and acceptance of others, especially those who could care less if he lives or dies, just as long as he gets their work done on time.

But now it's the weekend and look who's turning the corner walking with the **Hip Hop flava.** That's right! It's **Young Blood,** headed to his mom's house to chow down on her home made meatloaf and mash potatoes with a big jug of Kool-aid on the side. Don't worry folks this is only a temporary thing for **Young Blood**. Anyway, you better believe that the last thing on his mind is that high priced restaurant he ate in last night where the Filet Migon cost $90.00 a shot!

After dinner, the old crew stops by to shoot the breeze while knocking off some **Wild Irish Rose** and **Boones Farm Apple-Berry Wine,** laughing and joking like old times. Suddenly, it all comes to an end. You see, **Young Blood** has got to get back to the suburbs. He has to add some starch to his underwear so that he can be ready for his workweek with all those other stiff folks who possess no rhythm, and who also hide *undercover.*

The real shame is that **Young Blood** has a good heart; he's just not using it. This brother could do a world of good if he would share his secrets of success with some of the younger brothers who believe in making that quick and easy buck. Instead of teaching, **Young Blood** wants to criticize and place himself above others, so that he can continue to impress those he so desperately seeks acceptance from. **Young Blood** also knows that if he did do the right thing by giving back to his community, his co-workers would list him a troublemaker.

So **Young Blood** continues to follow the program and not rock the boat, and by doing this he has added his name to the list with the other brothers who have forgotten where they came from and who have also sold out their communities.

Such a shame.
Such a great lost.

IF I SHOULD DIE TONIGHT

I f I should die tonight, I want my family to know that I truly loved and respected them unconditionally. What few friends I have remaining, I have admired, envied loved and respected, also. I would not choose any other friends to go into battle with.

To my enemies:

You were admirable foes, worthy of the wars that were between us. You kept me on my toes and my mind sharp. But most of all, I leave these words to those who hated, disrespected and even refused to acknowledge me as a human being.

There were things in my past that I committed that I'm not proud of, but these are things that only my creator can judge and punish me for, not you. The negative feelings and or beliefs that I possess, I must also bear the burden of that responsibility. If there is any hate in my heart and soul, I want you to understand that hate was an action and feeling that was created by those who initiated the act. Now look into your mirror and tell me who you see.

Therefore, you must be held liable for this injustice. You must realize that you are the main contributor to this major wrong that my people and I are experiencing today, (remember the Willie Lynch project). It's inconceivable to think that someone could dehumanize, degrade and demoralize another simply because of their skin color. But the real truth is you hate yourselves for what you have become, which is barbaric, malicious and demonic. But there is another truth that you just refuse to acknowledge, and that truth is that you are part of us. Through your research you have found that my people are the true creators of history. This can no longer be denied.

So the next time that you or any of your people want to spurn someone else, do me a favor and look into your mirror first, and I'll bet that you will see the real perpetrator of the crime that you are trying to place upon someone else.

THE GAME PLAN

Obtain a thought that will lead to a goal.

Focus in on the most important parts of that goal that will bring it to life.

Remain positive, because there will be obstacles (mental and physical) that will try to   prevent you from reaching your destiny.

Work hard at your goal and allow it to manifest itself into reality,

    then all is done.

So remember **conceive, believe, succeed** then all will be **achieved.**

Collective Thoughts of a Black Man

FAILURE AND SUCCESS

Failure is nothing more than a form of success that you refuse to accept, because when one feels as though he/she is closing in on their goals they begin to think negative thoughts.

Therefore, the mind is placed in a situation whereas it can only react to accept failure as a way of life. This is a process that is taught to some to break the mind, body and soul. In order to break this process, one must feed his/her mind, body and soul, positive re-enforcement through living well.

Eliminate those in our lives who consistently want to pull us down to the gutter with them. Think positive by believing and saying to ourselves that there is nothing that I can't achieve. By not putting poison into our bodies. I'm not saying that if you want to have a drink occasionally, to stop, but do not allow alcohol or any other drug to take over your spirit and body to possess you in such a manner that you feel you can't do without them. These are foods that will allow the body to function as one complete unit; to excel past its negative boundaries to accept good and positive things.

Therefore, one should not look at failure as taking three steps backwards, but instead, look at failure as a concept of properly preparing yourself with a game plan that will lead you toward the great achievements that we all can have if we believe in ourselves.

THE PATHWAY
RETURNED

As I look back on certain moments and times of my life, I find myself walking the same path over again. I truly don't understand why. But there has to be a reason. In the past I would reject this path, but now I choose to follow it.

Maybe there is something in my past that I need to correct, or better yet, maybe there is something that I forgot to bring forth to the present that will help my future transitions become more stable and strong. Whatever it may be, I hope that this time as I walk this path my journey will continue to lead me toward my goals which are financial security, independence and happiness, but most of all, a piece of mind and a loving relationship with my God!

Collective Thoughts of a Black Man

WORDS AGAIN

Taken from freedom in **Africa**
Brought to captivity on the northern shores of **America**
From having a peace of **mind** and being a **whole man,** to having pieces of my **mind ripped,** and my **manhood stripped.**
I stood before many men being admired as a great **Warrior.**
Now I stand before many men awaiting the highest bid to become their working **Mule.**
I've worked this land and built many **Cities,** but I still don't own my
Forty Acres and a Mule.
You gave me books to read saying they would give me **knowledge.**
But when I look at these pages all I see is **lies** that continue to **brainwash** many to believe that all history was created by **White America.**
I was told that I have **Rights, both Civil and Human,**

But when someone can take away something that they claim you have
whose rights were they in the first place?
When living in **America** I'm told that I can be anything that I want to be,
a builder of great Cities and Nations, a Doctor to heal many people, even President to run the country.
Well, it seem to me, that before you crossed the ocean and brought the ships that many of us died on, and the chains to keep us tied down,
I was all of those things and more
without your approval.
You speak of **Freedom,** but how could this be.
Right after I'm born I'm given a number, (you call it a social security number). When I enter the work force I'm given a number (the employee or clock number) when I file for taxes or go to school I'm given a number. And you know damn well if you lock me up in prison I'm given a number.
Hell, if you lock a brother up over and over again, he's given quite a few numbers.
My point is all through life you know just where I am,
all you have to do is pull up that number,
So where is the **Freedom?**

JIVE TALKIN'
70s STYLE

My, My, girl. With that walk you know you need to be in another line of work. Sister you know you got it goin' on, you and yo' crew looking as fine as you wanna be with that long silky hair and that jet-black skin. Baby, I bet when you sweat you look like a dark chocolate candy bar meltin.' You know what, why don't you just melt all over me?

And looka here (pronounced like look-a) standing beside you. Baby girl, I know they done told you that you look like caramel, with that pretty smile and those big thighs. Now you know caramel is sticky, so why don't you let me get stuck on you for a few licks.

Whoa! Now who is this red bone right here, just as thick. Oooowe, girl I sho' would like to wrestle with you. Let me see if I can pin you 3 fo' 3 back at my crib. It's been a long time since a brotha has thrown out his back putting some work in, **YOU GAME?**

Hold-up, hold-up, you with these three sistas. Well, I'll be damn. Y'all done fooled around and added some Vanilla (in reference to a white girl) to the recipe. Now looka here Vanilla, I know if you are hangin' with these sistas, you got to have some flava in yo' soul, 'cause I can damn well see that you have the candy to make a sweet tooth hurt. Turn around and let me get a peek at you, Owww, as sugar foot from the Ohio Players would say. Girl did anyone ever tell you that you got a great future behind you? Damn vanilla, I know you make a chair happy when you sit down.

Y'all know what? Hell just fo' get it. It's time fo' me to go. I got to get my stroll on. But I will say this to all you sistas, **"KEEP IT REAL AND RIGHT ON TO YO,' RIGHT ON!" OH! AND LAWD HAVE MERCY....**

THE WALK OF PEACE

The journey to find God

My mind is forged within my solitude, destined to find the reasons of my eternal being. At times, my life has been like the ocean, shifting in many different directions; and like the ocean, with its waves crashing about and even coming to an abrupt stop, it seems as though my life has imitated this same pattern. My mind crashes and my body stops. If there is anyone watching at this moment, it may seem that I am pausing for a few seconds. To them, it may seem as though I'm contemplating a thought. But I know differently.

Those few seconds feel as if years are going by. My existence seems meaningless, and maybe it is. I use to worry about this plight in life, but not anymore. That's because when I'm awakened from this moment of darkness, I find myself standing in sand all alone, or at least I think I am alone.

Suddenly, my body and soul become calm. I feel inner peace. I look onto the sand and footprints become visible, yet there is no one around me. As these footprints begin to move, I hear a voice say, "Don't worry or fear. Just follow."

As I follow, I begin to ask questions. "Where am I going?" "Who are you?" "Why are you here?" "Why should I continue to follow this invisible being?" A few seconds go by without an answer. Then I hear his calm, but reassuring voice say again, "Don't worry or fear, just follow." And so I did. After a while I became really calm and at peace; no worries or fears. It seemed as though I was evolving; that my mind and soul had risen to another level. A level for which I had no knowledge, but yet, I felt prepared. Then suddenly the footprints had stopped. As I looked about, I could swear that I was in the wilderness, but the fact is I was somewhere. As I stood in the sand, other footprints then moved beside me. I heard a very soft, yet powerful, voice speak to me. *"I give life. I give joy and happiness. I give the greatest love to all who seek me. Even when you have sorrow in your heart, I give strength. My child, I give guidance and direction.* Then, the voice paused, allowing me to ask this one and only question? Then what do I do to receive these wonderful gifts? The voice replied, **"DON'T WORRY OR FEAR; JUST FOLLOW....."**

LOVE LETTER # 1

I've made love to you a thousand times; on a train, on a plane, in the park and in every place that my mind could imagine or conceive. To kiss, touch and caress every inch, and curve of your body, is a wonderful joy. To be deep inside of you. To hear the pounding of your heart. To feel the heat from your rapid breathing. To know, with every movement or position we take, our bodies are in sync; one beautiful and intense rhythm flowing like the ocean.

When the morning sun awakens me, the beauty of the day cannot measure up to you. That's because I know that Allah has given me his greatest creation, **YOU**. When I'm asked to describe you, the words Intelligent, Articulate, Strong, Bold, Brash, Sensual, Dynamic, and loving are used. You are a complete woman. Your beautiful hair, those sexy eyes, that glowing dark chocolate skin and that wonderful smile captivate me when I see you. You are my Queen placed upon the highest pedestal to be admired and respected.

You are my seconds, my minutes and my hours. You are my days, my months and my years. God is my lifeline and he has given you the abilities to become my immediate source of strength. You believe in me when no one else will, you love me in ways that many can't even begin to understand. If I have a picture in my mind that is unclear or the pathway to a resolution leads me in many different directions, just talking to you, I become focused again and the pathways become one. In the end, you don't ask for much, only my love, trust and belief in you. Well dear-heart I give you those things and so much more, because I know that if another day were to go by and The All Mighty Allah chooses not to give me anything else in life, that would be fine because he has given me more than I could wish for...

With All My Love,
SAEED

MEMORIES FROM THE HOOD

Good Times Gone, But Not Forgotten

When I was growing up, my neighborhood was probably like most. I knew a variety of characters. We had the church lady, the housewives, the street mechanics, winos, hustlers, pimps and prostitutes.

The people who had cars, drove everything from the old, beat up, last-leg cars, to the slick bad-ass Cadillacs and the Convertible Lincolns with the suicide doors (you know the ones with the front opening one way and the back doors opening the other way; maybe it was before your time).

Everybody knew somebody and everyone got along with one another. They gave respect to one another regardless of the type of living they made because whatever they did was their business. Everyone in the hood knew the church lady because when you walked by her house, you would speak to her and she would reply with a "God bless you." That was your cue to pick up your pace because you knew the next question was going to be, "When the last time you been to church boy?" I always got caught up in that long ass sermon on how I was the devils child, but still I loved the church lady.

The housewives were always nice. They would ask you to go to the store for them, and allow you to keep the change. You know, as I look back, I seem to remember those housewives being fine as hell, and they were married to some of the ugliest brothers alive, but they, too, were cool. But what I remember most about those wives were the words they would have with the hookers. It seems to me that some of those wives were turning tricks themselves and cutting into the hooker's action. I'm just telling like it is.

And what about the street mechanic? You know, the brother who always had four or five cars jacked up at one time, and always one or two tools short of completing the job. I know you know the type-- fast-talking, jive ass brother who always pulled off that last minute miracle to get your car fixed, and all it would cost was $25.00, a pack of cigarettes and a

6-pack of Miller's Beer. It didn't matter what type of job he did. The end results and payment were the same.

Now let's get to winos. Every time I turned around, one of them would have some Boones Farm or Wild Irish Rose (red wine of course) in one hand, and in the other, a half lit cigarette telling lies about how they were in the war or how they once belong to a singing group called the Five Tops. But because they got all the women, the other members forced them to leave, then re-named the group the Four Tops. It's always funny how these so-called solo acts never seemed to make it. Anyway, the winos were even cool, besides they told funny stories.

Now, when it came to the Hustlers, these brothers were no joke! If they didn't like you, they would cut you in a heartbeat. These brothers always carried straight razors. Razors so sharp, that you could be cut-up and not bleed until you got home (no sh*t jack). On the other hand, if they liked you, man, you had it made. These brothers would teach you the tricks of their trade. With some, it was cards and dice, with others it was selling something they got from their booster (oh yeah, remember them). Anyway, I got to learn a few things since my uncle was a big time player. Boy, I was in like Flynn.

Then remember the all too famous "Numbers Man" who would pay a kid a couple of bucks to go down the street to pick-up the church lady's numbers. I guess he didn't want to hear that sermon either. (Funny how church lady could preach the Lord's word one minute, then cut a 6-way number down to a 3-way pay off the next.) Wonder if she's any kin to Rev. Ike? (Sorry Rev., I still got mad love for ya'.)

Finally, the ultimate player is the Pimp. Now, when you hear the old saying, "Pimpin' ain't easy," you know it's got to be true. First, a brother has to realize that he has this unique talent, the gift to be able to play with words. Second, he has to be a visionary to get a woman to see and believe the picture that stands before her could in fact make her life easier if she would follow his program. Third, he has to be convincing enough to make her believe that he really cares for her in order to make his game tight! Fourth, this brother has to be the peacekeeper and the law at the same time, cause you know damn well if he has a large stable of women he has to keep harmony between them. The last component of being a good Pimp is the gift of sight and taste. You see, a pimp has to have women that look good and be built-up like a brick shipyard, and he has to have flava, Black women, White women, Asian, Latino, and so on. He has to have women who also have game, (not as tight as his) because she has to charm the "Tricks."

So when it all comes together, this brother can sit back in his long pretty hog (that's Cadillac for all you lames and saps who didn't know) and let the dead Presidents flow.

Now, I know that I didn't talk about a lot of other people, such as the honest, hard working people who also lived in my neighborhood; and believe me there were quite a few, they also played an important part in my upbringing. I wanted you to see that in my hood everyone was important, no matter their occupation. They gave respect and they got respect, no demeaning anyone, or placing anyone above anyone else--the playing field was always level.

I miss those days and the people because what we have today is just a very cheap version of yester-year. So that's it. I hope you enjoyed the trip through my old hood. I just hope yours was just as fun... **PEACE!!!**

LOST

I see you hiding among the others, wondering what direction to follow. That's your first problem. You want to follow instead of lead. Yeah-yeah. I know the old saying, "There are too many chiefs and not enough Indians." Well my brother, this is different. We need more Black men to step-up. To do many different things, such as being fathers to their children, husbands to their wives and positive role models to those who watch them closely. We need brothers to become teachers, not just in the classroom, but outside in the community. We need to reclaim our younger brothers and sisters.

As I walk the streets, I see and hear young people who live in a state of disillusionment, not believing the fact that they are the cause of this first stage of **GENOCIDE;** nor do they want to face their greatest challenge, **LIVING.** For them, there is no tomorrow, so they live life in a reckless way. Some young people cannot give love because they have not received or been taught how to love. Their belief system has been shattered by images of false success and quick riches. But I don't blame them, not completely.

We are the blame. That's right, you and me. You roll down the street in your Benz, Jag or BMW, not even attempting to come to a stop. You just want everyone to be able to get a quick glance at your symbol of success. Now don't get me wrong, I'm not hating on you because you're living large. I'm sure that your ride is a just and due reward for going to school and working hard at your craft. More power to you brothers and sisters. What I do hate is the fact that you want to keep the keys and tools to your success a secret. Why not share your gift? I know that you have a little time on your hands where you could stop in on your old school or neighborhood and share with the young people what it took to get where you are today. The fact is, if they could see, touch and talk to one of their own, it could make a big difference.

Now as I said earlier it's not just you, it's also me. I'm probably the guiltier of the two of us. That's because I'm still here in the mix of things. I may not be as successful as you are, but I do okay. The truth is, I sometimes get so angry and frustrated at these brothers and sisters, I just stop trying to talk to them, and that's wrong! When I get this attitude, I'll even say, "Forget it! If they want to kill themselves, let them. I've got my own life." You know what, that's truly f*cked up and I know better.

If it were not for those brothers who took the time out of busy lives to sit, talk and teach me, I would be in the same position, **UNEDUCATED and CRIMINAL MINDED** with dark dreams of **HOPELESSNESS and DESPAIR.**

I see these brother/sisters everyday. I have no excuse. Every time I see one of them doing wrong, I should do something to prevent it. I know and understand what they don't, and that is this process is unconsciously taught to them. When you grow-up with very little guidance, love and discipline you tend to have these thoughts, "If he can do it, and get away, I know that I can get over like a fat champ," or this thought, "She's got a little game, but sh*t I'm nickel slick and I know I could play the world for a fool." These are the things they've heard or possibly caught a quick glance at their parents doing, who watched their parents before them. The sad and tragic reality is that they never get over. They only sometimes get by, and that's until life pulls that fifth ace from the deck dealing that Bull-Sh*t that it has to offer them, leaving them with that feeling that life is over.

I would sit on my front steps and watch people walk down the street and try to read the expressions on their faces. Sometimes, I would be wrong and sometimes I knew that I was right on point! For example, I would watch this one young brother walk down the street and you could almost see these words across his forehead, "I'm going to crack the first sucka I see up-side his/her head and take what I can get." Well, he did just that. One night he decided to rob a neighborhood store, after clocking the owners wife in the head with a pistol, the owner himself came from the back of the store and blew that brother's back out with a 12-gauge shotgun. Well, I guess you know there will be no more mind reading, at least with that brother. Now we've got two lives lost, one because the brother who is dead should have had some sort of positive out-let to show him that life does have much to offer, if we only apply ourselves.

The second life lost is the store owner who came out to protect his wife, only to find out because he shot someone in the back, (who probably would have killed them both anyway) he will now have to face a screwed-up judicial system that will lock him up for life (Now you tell me where is the justice).

I guess what I'm saying to the both of us is that it only takes a few ticks of the clock to do something that will be rewarding, not only to the people that we inspire, but to ourselves. I leave you with these words, "If by planting the seeds of **Hope, Strength and Positive Affirmation through use of Direct Confrontation** we can then watch new young dynamic leaders grow tomorrow and the future beyond that."

PLEASE LET'S WAKE-UP...

I GOT MY JONES ON

Oh yeah, I'm feelin' real nice, mellow, and laid back. Man I just took a hit of the greatest stuff that was grown on this earth. Hold up! I got to get my drink on, too. Damn, that went down smooth. What this? Brothers and Sisters, this is the best that money can't buy. More than a 100 proof and fulfilling to the soul. Oh, now you want some. I knew it, with yo' greedy self, but it's okay. I got more than enough. Now pass me those Zig Zags. Yep, these are the good papers now pass me the bag.

What's in the mix of my special blend, **pride, self-respect, honor and a lot of perseverance, along with love for your family and your people.** Now we roll this up nice and tight. (Remember only use two pieces of paper; anymore will spoil the effects of the product.) Let's put some heat to this. Here, you take the first hit. Damn son, it's puff-puff pass, not puff-puff stash. Don't be like that. This is something you share with all the brothers and sisters. You don't keep this to yo' self.

Now you ready for that drink. While I pour, you take a couple more hits. Here you go, straight up, no chaser. Yeah, boy! Strong ain't it, but smooth. What is it? This is something that my grandmother use stir up in the bathtub when she was doing some bootleggin' back in the day. She then passed it down to my moms. Now, I'm sharing it with you. First, you pour in some **Determination** (to over come all adversities), add some **Morals** (to know and choose right from wrong), **Strength** (mental, physical and spiritual). Now, you stir it up and let it age a while, until you get what you have here in the glass.

A toast, "To all them that sacrificed for all of us." Damn Scout, you killed that off quick. Here take another one, but this time sip it nice and slow, allow it to be absorbed into your system. This is for life. That's why this drink is called the **Essence of Life**. Now, how do you feel? Yeah, I know. I know. Now take the rest of the bottle and the bag, share it with some of our other brothers and sisters, and watch how it affects them. Why! You still have to ask? I want us all to get our **"JONES ON."**

PUFF-PUFF PASS...

LOVE JONES

D amn I've got it bad! I can't eat, can't sleep or even think right. Man she's got me going in circles. She said she could do it. She said that she was going to make me love her.

Let me tell you how it all began. It was a beautiful summer day and I was at the park just chillin,' looking out onto the water. I had no special thoughts running through my mind, just enjoying the day when, suddenly, this drop dead beautiful sister walked up to me and asked the time. Brothers, as I turned towards her to reply, I looked upon the perfect woman. She was a tall drink of water, around 5'10 or 5'11. Thick in all the right places, she had on some short pants that would make a brother cry. Big calves, great thighs, hips and a butt that was the greatest of all wide receivers.

As my eyes traveled upwards, the rest of her just got even better. As I looked her in the eyes, I couldn't believe how beautiful she was. Then she spoke. As I watched her perfect full lips move, I became absorbed by the things that she said. I knew then, that I had to ask this sister for her number.

Well, some time has gone by and the more that I talk to her, the deeper I fall for her. Check this, here is a sister who is socially conscious about the welfare of her people; a sister who seeks equality, civil and human rights for our race. A strong, intelligent and articulate Black Queen, a sister who told me that she was down with the Black man. What was really hard hitting was when she said, "I'm in the fight for life, and when I stand with my man I have come to the conclusion that I would rather die with him than live without him."

Now brothers and sisters, that is deep. We've spent a lot time together, each moment becoming more intense. She's the kind of woman that keeps me in that thinking mode. One night, we were listening to an Old School station, the candles were burning and Marvin Gaye's song, *Sexual Healing*, was playing. Then, all of a sudden, she leaned over and kissed me. Afterwards, she said, "My strong Black Brother, I'm going to make you Love me." I knew then, I was in trouble. I thought about getting up to leave, couldn't make that move; we were at my house.

As she began to speak again, the Isley Brothers began to play. Now, you know when and if any Isley tunes are playing, especially slow songs, the next thing to happen is some serious Earth Shaking, Baby Making Last breath taking, love sessions. Yes, I said sessions - as in plural. Anyway, thank God, the tune playing was, *Fight the Power.*

Well, it was time for her to go. She had to leave so that she could prepare for work. A few weeks went by and we were out to dinner. I could tell that there was something wrong, so I asked, and without any hesitation, she told me that she was leaving. Her job was sending her to Seattle for good. I just sat there. I couldn't believe this. I felt ripped up and angry. Just when I allowed myself to become at ease with someone, it seemed as though she was being snatched right from me.

Days went by and I really didn't feel like doing anything. I just went to the park and looked into the water, hoping that I could re-create that first day when I had met her. Instead, I realized something else. I had a **love jones**. I found myself searching and thinking constantly about this woman, contemplating the thought of marriage. Sharing my life with this Exotic and Erotic person who could set my soul on fire; who could show me passion one moment, and in the next, she's ready to go to war beside me. Damn, how could this happen?

Well, she's gone and I haven't talked to her, but as I lie in my bed sometimes listening to that Old School station playing David Ruffin, Barry White, Harold Melvin & the Blue Notes, I think of her. Then I smile as I begin to fall asleep. In the end, I ask, why couldn't this have been? My answer came from inside my soul. We only think we are ready for something or someone to come into our lives; the truth is we're not! Only Allah (GOD) knows when we are ready, and when he feels that the time has come to give us his special gifts, then he will place them before us. So until then, I'll wait patiently for my Queen. And when she's arrives, I will kneel before her feet and pay homage to her and to the greatest gift giver of the universe, the almighty **ALLAH.**

Collective Thoughts of a Black Man

TURNED OUT

The Story of a Fallen Angel

S o you think you've done something. Yeah right! You think that you are a big man. You think that since you have suckered this sister into buying your dope and now she is strung out, you are a real player. Yeah, right. Back up off her, I said back up mutha f*cka before I let off two to your skull. I am not going to let this sister fall. Yeah, just keep walking cause I'll see you another day.

Come on sister, let's get you some help, let's get you right. Baby girl, what happened? I know that it's tough out here. I realize you are alone with the feeling of not being loved. I also realize that there are many times when others just don't seem to care about your problems because they have many of their own, but sister that's no reason to stick a needle in your arm or smoke some stuff that could bring an elephant down. Don't keep giving your body up as a trade for drugs, just to escape reality for a few moments. Yo' man? What about your man? Was that him back there feeding you this poison while going upside you head at the same time? Sister he's not your man; he's just a provider of **DEATH.** Besides he's not even a man, he's a punk-bitch brother and he'll get his, trust me!! Look here Queen, yes, I said Queen. You don't need no man, friend or family member that would allow you to do this to yourself. You also don't need anyone who would sell, give or allow you to sample products as a human lab rat. We've got enough of that bull-sh*t going on with the government.

My sister, sometimes we must face life's greatest challenges alone. It's those battles that makes us strong and give us insight on what's ahead. If we can overcome our adversities alone, then think how easy it will be with even the slightest amount of help.

You have so much to offer, don't give up. After you've gotten yourself back together, you can help other sisters who have walked that same dark path. You must help prevent this madness.

(Time has gone by.)

Well, well look at you sister, healthy, beautiful and strong with a clear and focused goal. Everything is going to be right in the universe.

Please just stay on track, my sister. Much love and respect to you, but now I've got some business to 'tend to.

Moments later, a brother approaches me and asks if I had some loose change. Just when I was about to give him the change, I had to do a double take.

"Yo' man, look at me." "So you want some change, huh?" "You remember me?!" "No, just as well, because today you are one lucky brother."

By now, I guess you're wondering, "Who is this brother?" Well, remember the brother who was feeding his poison to the **Fallen Angel** when I came along? It seems as though he has become a **product** of his own **product;** instead of being the seller, he is now the user. Good! That serves his bitch-ass right, because I was coming to put an end to his reign. But, as usual, the right power intervened and brought along the proper justice. He's lucky Satan and his madness got a hold of him first, cause I was going to send him to Hell anyway. Now he's got to face a far worse punishment, **living in the belly of the beast,** a self induced Hell; a pit that has taken so many good brothers and sisters; a black hole that hasn't taken enough of the bad brothers and sisters.

P. S.

To all my Brothers and Sisters let's stop the madness. We can overcome any and everything if we would just wake-up, WAKE-UP, **WAKE-UP!**

LET ME SOFT-N THE BLOW

So you want to keep injecting yourself with Ignorance and Stupidity. Then, take this - pop, pop, pop, pop - four shots to your dome! And you, still collecting those welfare checks and having these babies. Then take these - wop, wop - two quick brain shakers, a left and right hook.

My young brother would you come a little closer. So you think it's cool to wear your pants hanging off your butt. Cool then take this – bap! Damn that felt good, I cracked his skull down to the white meat. I've got to remember that punch, a straight jab to the center of the head.

Hey you! Come here! I said come here! Don't make me chase you! Oh, you're going to run anyway.

Now that I've caught you listen up. Why do you use drugs? I don't care if it's only a couple joints. Okay then, take this Cranium Check - tap, tap, tap – Oh, wait a minute - pop, pop, pop. "Why did I go upside your head six times?"

Well the first three were for inhaling that stuff, and the next three, well, I figured that you were too high to realize that I had already hit you the first three times.

My mistake playa, I guess you got a bold bag. You should have been mellow by now.

By now, all of you are probably wondering why they call me the **Cerebral Assassin.** Well, somebody has to wake you up.

First my brother, pick up a book, get an education, or possibly learn a trade. Opportunities are not given; they are made or taken by the person who created them in the first place.

Now, you sister. There isn't a brother alive who would get involved with a woman who has six or more babies, unless he was trying to get you to max out your Bridge Card to feed his four kids. Think about it, you will run a hard working brother away after he sees the bill for all those Happy Meals that he's got to pay for.

And you my misty-eyed young brother; do you really think that Puff-Daddy is walking around with his pants hanging off his behind. Hell No! That brother is wearing his own designs, along with Prada, Gucci, Hugo Boss, Cerrutti and Armani topping them off with some Big Block Crocks, (what can I say I like my clothes). Now, get up from in front of the B.E.T. channel, go and get a job. Oh, pull up those pants, and while you're at it change your underwear they don't look so white.

It finally comes down to you. Hey, brother, I said I was sorry for those last three blows. Anyway, why are you burning up your brain cells? I'm sure that you've got some sort of talent that you could put to use. Say brother, do you hear me talking? Wait a minute. I know these signs glass eyed stare, no verbal communication or body language, **ZONED OUT!** Well folks I guess we've lost this one, you can take him of the fire heeeee's done.

To you remaining three, the blows that I gave you are nothing compared to life's hits. You've got to be ready, Minister Malcolm X once said, "Of all our studies, history is best qualified to reward our research." And last I say, "The world is a ghetto, but does it mean that it's people have to be **GHETTO FABULOUS**?

I'm done talking now. Somebody take this other brother to rehab before the buzzards start circling him.

Collective Thoughts of a Black Man

THE PIMP'S RAP

I can make a wet dream dry.

I can make the finest of all women sit down and cry.

I can make a Housewife tell you the most believable lie.

Without this Strong and Intense Chocolate lovin,' she would lie down and die.

I'm **The Pimp** of all Pimps, **The Player** of all Playas and **The Mack** of all Macks.

Listen up, listen tight, I'll keep you close, for right now. I'll even keep you on tap, but When it's time to move on

Baby don't get upset;

Just realize that you were another victim of

THE PIMP'S RAP.

MOTHER EARTH AND FATHER TIME

One day, while sitting in the park, I began watching people as they went about their ways. Some seemed as though they were moving faster than the speed of light, while others were moving as slowly as possible, without a care in the world. I watched a lot of couples do, I guess what couples do. But there was one couple that received more of my attention than the rest. Some would describe this couple as mature or senior citizens; I prefer to use "seasoned vet," due to the fact that during their years on this planet I'm sure they have experienced a lot.

As this couple made their way toward the water I noticed how the elderly male held his lady's hand, walking with her by his side with so much pride that it was truly amazing. They would gaze upon the water, and then look at one another. I could see smiles and hear laughter. As he leaned over to kiss her, I felt a warm sensation in my often-cold heart. I think, at times, I had the nerve to be jealous. I don't know what made me do it, but I decided to approach this couple. As I walked toward them, I could see the gentleman putting himself in position, between me and his lady, like a guarded stance. I began to smile and the thought going through my head was, "Here in his golden years this Warrior still protects his Queen."

After finally getting close to them and showing that I presented no harm, I introduced myself and we began a conversation. We talked about many things; History, especially Black History. We talked about the role of the black male and his family; and the role of the Black woman, and how she is many times neglected. We talked about what the future holds or could hold for our people. We talked about so many interesting things that there was a moment where I dropped my head in a state of amazement. The lady who had notice me lowering my head then asked what was wrong. I paused, and then said, "I don't know what brought me over to you, but I'm glad I came." The man had now placed his aged, but still strong hand on my shoulder and said to me, "Son, whatever it was that brought you here, meant for it to be." He continued, "I see that you are a big, strong man, and you also possess intelligence and pride, but your greatest strength is your Heart & Soul." As he extended his hand to say goodbye, his lady walked up to me with her arms wide open and gave me a loving embrace and imparted her wisdom upon me. As we embraced I could feel the passage of time; from the hardships to the days of glory.

She said to me, "I know that you have made mistakes in your life and you're going to make many more, just accept them and move on." She continued by saying, "I know what brought you over here. It was God." She said he had sent me their way for two reasons: first, to show respect and I did. The second was to learn what they both had to teach me.

I said that I often feel hard and cold. She replied, "Don't worry; you are only protecting yourself and the one's you love." She placed her hand on my chest and said, "Young Lion, inside the massive chest beats an even larger heart. I know this because I know that you are one of God's Soldiers." She walked away with her king.

As I look back upon that day, I have to give praise to almighty Allah for his gifts of **knowledge,**

respect and love and I received these gifts from the greatest of all people, a truly and sincerely respected and admired elderly Black couple who I saw as **MOTHER EARTH AND FATHER TIME.**

SOUL OF THE PANTHER

Ever since I can remember, my mother use to say, "Son you are too out spoken!" Even when I was a very little boy, I had no problems expressing myself on how I felt about certain issues, especially those concerning race. I learned very early in life what it was to experience a dislike for someone just because of his skin color or because one holds a certain belief.

When it came down to showing how much pride I have for those that I considered my heroes, man, you should have seen how fast I could clear a room. As I grew older, around the age of 11 or 12, I noticed that my thoughts were much different from those of my friends; the way I processed something in my mind and the way I was able to translate it to people. When I was in school, I noticed that when my teachers would discuss Black history, they only spoke of the Black leaders who were considered to be the **Safe Negro Leaders.** People who didn't believe in becoming too radical; the non-violent Negro who was considered to be less of a threat to this so-called American society. My teachers would always talk about people like Dr. Martin L. King, Jr., Dr. Charles Drew, Dr. George Washington Carver, and so on. Do you see where I'm going? Not to discredit any of these wonderful people, I give much love and respect to them all, but the simple fact is I just got bored learning the same things about the same people year after year, especially from teachers who played it just as safe, so they would not rock the boat.

But I was different. I knew that I was radical and controversial, so I took it upon myself to study and learn about people that would play a major role in my life to this present day, people like: Minister Malcolm X, Congressman and Rev. Adam Clayton Powell, Jr., The Most Honorable Elijah Muhammed, The Honorable Louis Farrakhan, and Frederick Douglass. Groups such as The Black Panther Party; events in history such as the murders of Emmett Till, Medgar Evers, Fred Hampton; and deliberate cruelties like The Tuskegee Experiment. Now do you see where I'm at!

These were brothers and groups that changed history in one way or another; most of them challenged the status quo, and so do I. Now I don't want you to think that I was some sort of child prodigy. I'm far from that. I enjoyed most of my childhood when I could. I participated in sports, but I learned that some of **white** America looked at black athletes as entertainers to amuse them for their pleasure. (If you doubt this, research and find out how many black general managers are in the ranks of pro sports, then find out how many are the sole owners of any of these teams.

I knew that I wanted to be someone who set himself apart from others, if not economically, then socially. I realize there are a lot of people who feel the way I do, but that's where we differ. Most of these people know where I'm coming from, and they have experienced the many harsh realities of life, but for some reason or another, they choose to remain silent. Not me. I'm going to tell it like it is - direct and brash, and if it hurts your feelings, then next time you'll think twice before coming off the porch to run with the BIG DOG.

It's plain and simple. If you hit me, I'm going to hit you back. If you disrespect me or my loved ones, then I'm going to put fear in your heart and soul. On the other hand, if you want to sit and have an intelligent conversation with me about my concerns, about my race and culture, then we may do so in the most civil way. I just want you to understand that the man you approach is just that, a man; born FREE. What I mean by this statement is, I have no constraints, mentally or physically. I will not be denied in any way my respect as a man, nor any pleasures that I may seek. I will go where I want, do as I please and say what's on my mind without having to feel that I have to explain myself to anyone the actions I may take.

What I want you to know is that I have the **Soul Of The Panther** burning deep inside of me. I am *intelligent, articulate*, and *well informed*. So America, I want you to realize that I am one of the most dangerous men you may encounter. If you have any notions of trying any trickery, beware because when I hold court, you will be held accountable for all crimes that you have thrust upon The Black people for the last 440 years; and trust me you will be found **GUILTY.**

Long Live The Panther...

THE AUTHOR'S EXIT

Brothers and Sisters, we all have individual purposes for being here on earth. Some of us were blessed with that specific purpose, while the rest must wait until Allah (God) gives that supreme plan. But until then, let us all focus in on the one main gift that we should be sharing, and that is **UNITY!!**

I conclude with a quote from The Most Honorable Elijah Muhammed, "If we want whites or other Blacks to respect us, we must clean and wash ourselves of the filth in and out; we must first be brothers."

**As-Salaam Alaikum
(May Peace Be Upon You)**

CLOSURE

"Give instructions to a wise man and he will yet become wiser: Teach a just man, and he will increase in learning."

Proverbs 9:9
The Holy Bible

ABOUT THE AUTHOR

Saeed Muhammed was given the name Charles E. Giles at birth. Born and raised in Detroit, Michigan, Mr. Muhammed is a product of the Detroit Public Schools. He graduated from Mackenzie High School and attended Wayne State University where his studies focused on the social and economic conditions of African Americans in America.

Muhammed's personal and professional life are just as intense as his writings. Growing up in tough neighborhoods with very tough friends and foes forced him to prove his toughness by not giving in to the negativity that the streets would provide.

Muhammed has 20 years of experience in and throughout the criminal justice system by working in the private and public sectors of Law Enforcement and by being an entrepreneur. He is a professional bodyguard, certified bounty hunter and co-owner and creator of a clothing line that represents the Black experience. He has covered the many different spectrums of his still young life.

When asked, "What is yet to come," the author replied, "Within the powers that I control, to make sure that my family is safe, secure and happy, for I cannot control wherever it is that Allah wants me to be."

Wherever it is that Mr. Mahammed's life may lead him, this strong, brash and intelligent brother should keep writing.....

STAY TUNED............